Dain

This book will be of use to those who wish to keep a dainty table without incurring any extravagance.

The recipes are extremely varied and a great point is made of serving and garnishing prettily. This can sometimes be overlooked by the ordinary cook.

DAINTY DISHES
FOR SLENDER INCOMES

A book of advice

Copper Beech Publishing

Dainty Dishes for slender incomes

Published in Great Britain by
Copper Beech Publishing Ltd
© Copper Beech Publishing Ltd 2002

ISBN 1-898617-34-1

'Dainty Dishes for Everyday Use' picture used courtesy of Nestlé UK Ltd.

A CIP catalogue record for this book is available from The British Library.

Copper Beech Gift Books
Copper Beech Publishing Ltd
P O Box 159 East Grinstead
Sussex England RH19 4FS

FROM THE DAINTY HOUSEWIFE'S NOTEBOOK ...
WELL-TRIED RECIPES
FISH
MUTTON
BEEF
PORK
POULTRY
GAME
SOUP
VEGETABLES
SAUCES
SWEET DISHES
HINTS WORTH REMEMBERING

From The Dainty Housewife's Notebook...

Laying the Table

Lay the table daintily - it costs no more to set a table properly than to fling the things on anyhow. Do not consider this unduly extravagant with table-cloths and serviettes, for even the daintiest and most delicately cooked meal in the world will not look appetising if served upon soiled table linen and accompanied by serviettes long past their pristine freshness.

WELL-TRIED RECIPES

Where economy is practised, sufficient scraps are often left from the various meals to furnish other meals and the usual family soups and broths without buying fresh for the purpose.

A thrifty cook will inspect her larder each morning, and will put aside all cooked and raw bones of meat, game and poultry, drops of gravy, sauces, spoonfuls of vegetables, macaroni &c., and will use them either for the stockpot or to help finish off some stock already to hand.

Thrifty

Soup can be prepared from meat, game, or poultry, cooked in water or milk, with every kind of vegetable, sweet herbs, spices, curry powder &c., to give them flavour and seasoning.

Fish **FISH IN WHITE SAUCE**

Remove from the bones any white boiled fish left from the previous day's dinner, and break into convenient sized pieces. Set aside. To the bones, heads, tails and fins, add a small onion, a sprig of parsley, a small blade of mace, and a pint of water. Let it simmer in a pan by the fire till the liquid is reduced by half and then strain the stock through a sieve. To this fish stock, add a quarter of a pint of cream, or half milk and half cream, thicken with a little flour and butter, season to taste. Warm the pieces of fish in this sauce.

Hint: Do not let the sauce boil, or it will curdle.

Put a border of nicely mashed potatoes around your dish, and serve up the fish and sauce quite hot.

TO DRESS FISH A SECOND TIME

To a small quantity of fish, add two handfuls of bread crumbs, two eggs, two ounces of butter, a little essence of anchovy, and a little pepper, salt, and cayenne. Mix these all well with the fish, which should previously be taken from the bones and pounded; butter a plain mould, put in the mixture, and steam it until it is hot through.

Any cold boiled fish may be dressed in this way.

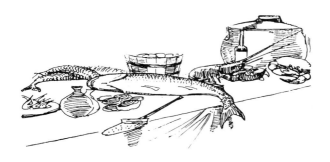

From The Dainty Housewife's Notebook...

To Keep Parsley
Don't follow the usual plan and put it in water. Instead, put it in an air-tight tin. It will keep double as long.

Valuable Water
The water in which fresh meat or vegetables have been boiled, is most valuable as a foundation for soups. It contains the nutritious parts and flavour of the food cooked in it.

FISH CAKES

To about a pound of cold boiled fish, either salt or fresh, add one and a half pounds of mashed potatoes; beat well together in a mortar with the addition of an egg and a little milk, and season with salt, pepper, onions, and a little thyme well chopped; of course, omitting the salt if the fish should have been salted. Then with a little flour, roll into small round cakes, rather thick, and fry a light brown. Dish them up as you would cutlets.

Hint: Frying in deep fat is more economical than the ordinary method beloved of English cooks; also, food cooked in this way has a far daintier appearance than that which has been subjected to the ordeal of an ordinary frying-pan.

CURRIED COD

Boiled cod makes an excellent réchauffé as a curry. For about a pound of fish, free from skin and bones, take the following ingredients:- two ounces of butter, one ounce of curry powder, six ounces of finely chopped onions, and two salt-spoonfuls of salt. Melt the butter in a stewpan, then add the curry powder, onions, and salt, and let them boil thoroughly, or the curry powder will taste raw; put in the pieces of cod broken into large flakes, and let them cook for five minutes over an established fire, keeping it constantly stirred to prevent burning. If the curry seems too dry when the fish is added, pour in a little milk, just sufficient to moisten it without making it liquid.

Pile the curry high in a dish, and serve with a border of well-boiled rice round it.

Over an established fire

FISH AND MACARONI

Take the remains of any kind of white boiled fish, remove the bones and skin, and break it in rather small pieces. Boil some macaroni in water till tender, drain it well, and cut it in lengths of about an inch, and mix equal quantities of fish and macaroni. Then put two ounces of butter into a stewpan, add the yolks of two eggs, a little lemon juice, pepper, and salt, and stir in well half a pint of good melted butter; make the sauce quite smooth, put in the fish and macaroni, and heat it thoroughly in the sauce.

Pour it out on a dish, keeping it as high as you can in the centre, cover it thinly with fine bread crumbs, and brown the top with a salamander or in the oven till a nice light colour.

FISH PUDDING

mashed potato

Take equal quantities of any cold boiled white fish and mashed potatoes. Break the fish up quite small, and mix well with the potatoes, adding two ounces of butter made liquid in the oven, or if you have it, you may use cream instead of the butter; season with salt and a little pepper.

Butter a pudding dish, put in the mixture, keeping the top rough, and place it in the oven till hot through and the top is nicely browned.

Money-saving Ideas
—

To abstain from small
extravagances is the
secret of making money
go further.

COD FRITTERS

Take the cod from the bones in large flakes. Make a batter of the proper consistency for frying, of flour, a little salad oil, a small quantity of light white wine, and a little salt. Dip the flakes of cod in this batter, fry them in boiling fat, drain well, and serve.

KEDGEREE

Boil a teacupful of rice, take cold whiting and pick all the meat from the bones; mix two ounces of butter with the rice first, then the fish, seasoning with pepper, salt a little cayenne, and lastly, add two eggs beaten slightly, stir all together over the fire quickly for a minute or two, and serve hot.

Hint: This is an excellent dish for breakfast.

Mutton **GRILLED CUTLETS**

Cut the slices of mutton rather thick, and make
them of the same form and size; warm them in a
good flavoured thick sauce, then dip them into fine
bread crumbs, then into yolk of egg in which you
have beaten a little very finely chopped parsley and
onion, then again into the bread crumbs; grill them
over a slow fire, and serve them up with a little
clear brown gravy.

HASHED MUTTON WITH MUSHROOMS

Cut the mutton into nice slices and dredge each slice on both sides with flour. Take six good sized mushrooms, trim them, cut each into four pieces, put into a pan with a small piece of butter to stew; add a little good stock and some pepper and salt; later, put in the meat; let it heat through slowly, stirring frequently to prevent burning.

Hint: Be careful that it does not boil, or the meat will be hard.

As soon as the flour loses its raw taste and thickens the hash, it is done, and should be served immediately with sippets of neatly cut thin toast or fried bread round the dish.

MUTTON PUDDING

Good pudding may be made from cold mutton; boiled is better for the purpose than roast, but either may be used. Cut the mutton in rather thick; mix well together in a plate some flour, salt, and pepper with a good sized onion finely chopped, and into this mixture dip each piece of mutton; slice three or four potatoes. Then butter a pudding mould or basin, line it with a light suet crust, lay in lightly the mutton and potatoes in alternate layers till you have filled up your mould. Pour in a teacupful or more of good stock, cover the top closely with the rest of the suet crust, and boil or steam it till done.

MARROW STUFFED WITH MUTTON

Cut a good sized vegetable-marrow in half, down the length, scoop out the seeds, and fill with the following mixture:

Mince very fine a little cold mutton, dredge a little flour over it, season with pepper, salt, a little finely chopped onion, and bind together with yolk of egg. Fill the centre of the marrow with this, tie the two halves together with some fine packthread, and stew it till tender in good flavoured stock. When done, take it out of the stock, which you must thicken with the yolks of two or three eggs; pour this sauce over the marrow (from which you have previously removed the string) and serve.

Hint: If you prefer it, you may use several small marrows instead of one large one.

HASHED BEEF

Beef

Cut as much cold roast beef as you require for your dish in neat slices, free from skin and gristle. Put into a stewpan a small piece of butter, a large onion minced, a table-spoonful of flour, and keep stirring over the fire till it browns, but be careful it does not burn. Then stir in by degrees half a pint of good flavoured stock, add salt to taste, and let the sauce boil till it thickens sufficiently, then put in two table-spoonfuls of hot green pickle chopped small, and the slices of beef; let them heat through, and serve with sippets of toast round the dish.

hot green
pickle

Fireproof Pot.

MINCED BEEF AU GRATIN

 Mince small as much cold roast beef as you need for your dish. Put into a stewpan a small quantity of good brown sauce, together with a shalot chopped small; salt, pepper, and nutmeg; give it a good boil, and warm the meat in this, making it rather thick. Pour it into a deep dish, cover it over thickly with fine bread crumbs, sprinkle over some oiled butter, and put it into the oven to brown nicely, and serve immediately.

Money-saving Ideas

—

**Keep an exact account
of every halfpenny
you spend.**

MEAT PATTIES

Line some patty pans with pastry. Fill with cold meat, minced and mixed with mashed potato. Add pepper and salt. Cover over the patties with thin pastry, press the edges together with a fork, make a hole in the centre. Bake till thoroughly cooked.

patty
pans

POTTED BEEF

Mince some cold boiled beef and then pound in a mortar with some fresh butter till quite smooth. Season with nutmeg, black pepper, cayenne, mace and salt. Press firmly into flat pots; clarify some fresh butter, pour over the top of each pot, and when cold, paper it over, and keep in a cold place.

Hint: The lean part of the meat is the best.

23

GALLIMAUFRY

Take as much cold salt beef as you require for your dish, and mince it small. Boil some cabbages till nearly done, take them out of the saucepan, drain the water thoroughly from them, and chop them small. Take equal quantities in bulk of the minced beef and cabbage, mix them well together, and fry with a little butter, or good clarified dripping, in a frying-pan till done of a nice light colour; pile the gallimaufry high in a dish, and serve very hot.

From The Dainty Housewife's Notebook...

When Blanching Almonds
An easy way to blanch almonds is to pour boiling water on them and let them stand for about ten minutes, when the skins will peel off quite easily.

How to Wash Glasses
If you want your tumblers and wineglasses to do credit to your dainty table, have them washed in this way: First in warm, soapy water, then rinse in cold, wipe as soon as possible with a clean, dry cloth, and polish with tissue paper.

Pork **MINCED PORK WITH ONIONS**

Mince some cold roast pork, but not too fine. Then slice very thin two large onions; put them into a stewpan with a little bit of butter to brown slightly, add three-quarters of a pint of stock, and let the onions stew well in it.

When done, put in three table-spoonfuls of brown sauce if you have it, if not, a little glaze or browning, salt, pepper, and thicken with a small quantity of flour and butter; boil well, and then add the minced pork; warm it in the sauce, and serve.

BREAKFAST FRITTERS

This recipe is very useful when the joint of cold
boiled ham is getting too shabby to appear and a
dainty dish is required. Cut neat slices of ham,
and dust lightly over with cayenne pepper. Make
a batter by thickening half a pint of milk and two
eggs with a cupful of flour; let this soak overnight.
Next day beat the batter again, dip each slice of
ham into it, and fry in lard.
Drain very dry, and serve on a hot dish with a garnish of chopped parsley.

**too
shabby**

Money-saving Ideas
—
No 'sundries' are admitted
as an item in well-kept
household accounts.

Poultry **QUENELLES OF TURKEY**

Take as much of the white meat as you require
from a cold turkey (keeping out the skin and sin-
ews), and pound it in a mortar; take half as much
in bulk of crumb of bread, soak it in milk, and add
with a small piece of butter; mix thoroughly and
pound all together, and put in the yolks of two or
three eggs, according to the quantity of the turkey
&c., some salt, pepper, a little nutmeg, and pound
the whole again. Next whip the whites of the eggs
to a stiff snow froth, mix them well and lightly
with the ingredients, and divide into small pieces,
to which you give the shape of little thick sausages,
dredge them with flour, fry them a light colour,
and serve piled high on a napkin, garnished with
sprigs of fried parsley.

PARSLEY.

fried
parsley

From The Dainty Housewife's Notebook...

Ample food

Tell your husband that he need never hesitate to bring a man home to dinner unexpectedly, say:

"There will always be a dainty dinner and
a dainty table."

Of course this is not easy at first, but once you are in the way of things, and can cut and contrive, there will always be an ample meal and to spare for at least four people.

GRILLED LEGS OF TURKEY

Pour melted butter over some cold turkey and sprinkle well with salt, pepper, and a little cayenne. Grill over a clear fire, and serve very hot with the following sauce round: take four large onions, peel them, and chop them rather small, put them into a stewpan with a little butter.

Let them fry to a good colour, but not black; then add more than half a pint of good flavoured stock, thicken with a little flour, stir in a dessert-spoonful of ready-made mustard, salt to taste, let the sauce boil well and skim it. As the last thing, add the juice of half a lemon.

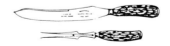

SCALLOPED CHICKEN

Cut some cold fowl into very small pieces, and put it into a stewpan with a little white sauce, or if you have not white sauce, a little stock, a table-spoonful of cream, and a little flour; season with salt and nutmeg; let it boil, stirring constantly, and when thick enough, fill your scallop shells with this preparation; cover them with fine bread crumbs, sprinkle over with some oiled butter, and brown the scallops in the oven or before the fire.

VOL-AU-VENT OF CHICKEN

Make a vol-au-vent case of the lightest puff paste, and fill it when baked with minced chicken, put a few button mushrooms stewed in white sauce on the top, and serve.

From The Dainty Housewife's Notebook...

To serve
Bread sauce, fried crumbs and gravy should
accompany all birds. Serve the gravy in a hot
tureen; never pour it over the birds.

FRIED CHICKEN

Cut a cold chicken into small joints, and put them in a deep dish, covering them with some chopped parsley, onion, salt, pepper, a little good salad oil, and squeeze over all the juice of a lemon; let the chicken remain in this for three or four hours, turning the pieces every now and then; then take them out, dredge over each piece with flour, and fry them.

Pile high on a dish, and pour the following sauce round:- put into a stewpan two or three table-spoonfuls of vinegar, according to the strength, a shalot minced, a small bay-leaf, a clove of garlic, salt, pepper, and half a pint of good stock, or the gravy from a roast joint; let the sauce boil well, skim the fat off, strain through a sieve, and use.

garlic

MAYONNAISE OF CHICKEN

Put some cold cooked chicken into a deep dish, add a little oil, vinegar, pepper, salt, chopped onion, and parsley. Cover the dish closely and leave for a few hours.

The sauce ...

Take the yolks of two hard-boiled eggs, pound them well, and mix with the yolk of a raw egg, a salt-spoonful of very finely chopped shalot, salt, white pepper, a little pounded sugar, add some good salad oil (a drop at a time or you will curdle the sauce if your pour it in too quickly) stirring it constantly. Moisten with a little tarragon vinegar, till you have sufficient sauce for your mayonnaise. The proportion of oil to vinegar is three of the former to one of the latter, and you must be guided by taste as to the quantity of salt, pepper, and onion. This sauce must be thick and highly flavoured, or when the cream is added it will be sloppy and tasteless.

The eggs ...

Boil six eggs for ten minutes, throw them into cold water and take off the shells. Cut a small slice from the wide end of each egg and then cut each into quarters lengthways.

The dish ...

Butter thickly a strip round the edge of a dish, and on this fix the quarters of egg upright and closely together, the white of the egg being outside. Inside this, put a layer of well dried and shredded cabbage lettuce. Fill in the centre with the drained chicken. Before serving, take a gill of good cream, whip it lightly, and mix carefully with the sauce and pour over. Serve at once.

Game   ## GAME PATTIES

Make as many patties of a small size as you require for your dish of good light puff paste, egg them over, and bake them until they are a nice light colour. Fill the centre with a mince of any kind of game; dish them on a napkin, and send to table quite hot.

PATTY-PANS, PLAIN AND FLUTED.

Money-saving Ideas
—

Prices should be compared
and lessons learned
from experience.

SALMI OF PARTRIDGES

Cut up what is left of cold partridges, and set aside
all the good parts: take what is left of the bones
&c., and pound them in a mortar and put into a
stewpan with a small piece of fresh butter, a shalot,
a bay-leaf, and some sprigs of parsley. Let all brown
a little, stirring constantly; then add a table-spoonful of flour, three-quarters of a pint of stock or both,
and a glass of white wine.

Let all boil slowly for some time, and when done,
strain through a sieve; warm the pieces of partridge
in this sauce, and serve with pieces of fried bread
round the salmi in the dish.

fried
bread

37

PARTRIDGE OR GROUSE SALAD

Cut up the cold bird into small-sized joints, and put into a deep dish; pour over four table-spoonfuls of good salad oil, one and a half of tarragon vinegar, and a table-spoonful of meat jelly; season with pepper, salt, and sprinkle with the following herbs chopped fine: equal quantities of parsley, tarragon, chives, and chervil. Let the pieces of meat remain in this mixture for two hours in a cool place, well covered over, then take them out and place them neatly on a layer of well dried shredded lettuce; decorate with pickled gherkins cut in small pieces, slices of hard-boiled eggs, fillets of anchovies, and savoury jelly cut in diamond shapes. Pour the mixture all over and serve.

From The Dainty Housewife's Notebook...

The Table-centre

A dainty table-centre need cost but a few pence
and if care is taken of it, and it is properly folded,
it will last for quite an indefinite time.

HOW TO START A STOCKPOT

Stock is a useful liquid that ought always to be ready for use in the kitchen. The foundation is water, into which the juices and flavour of meat, bones, and vegetables have been extracted by steady boiling.

Buy a special cast-iron, or copper stockpot, fitted with tap and strainer, or select a large, clean iron saucepan. Fill it two-thirds full of cold water, add a little salt, and then all suitable scraps available. During the day keep adding fresh bits, and keep the pot steadily boiling. It should boil from seven to eight hours a day.

Hint: The inferior parts of meat are quite suitable for soup making, and to buy the 'choice cuts' for this purpose is merely extravagant.

Every night:
Empty the stockpot, straining the liquid off into a clean basin. Wash and air the pot.

Next day:
Remove all fat from the liquid and pour it back into the pot. Either add fresh scraps or those which were strained out if there seems to be any nourishment left in them. If the liquid has been too much reduced, add more water.

Once a week, restart the pot with everything fresh.

Soup **CHOWDER**

Take two cods' heads, and boil them down in water to a thick soup. Wash and grate two middling sized carrots, and mix with sufficient powdered biscuit to thicken the soup (if you like you may add a captain's biscuit cut in slices), and flavour with sweet marjoram, summer savoury, two good-sized onions sliced, pepper, salt, and a little cayenne. Then slices of cod or haddock are to be put into the soup, and boiled twenty minutes before serving up.

ECONOMICAL POTATO SOUP

Cut a moderately sized breast of mutton into small pieces, and put it into three quarts of water; make it boil, skim it carefully, and season the broth with pepper and salt to your taste. Peel and cut into quarters six large and sound potatoes and three turnips, slice up four onions and three heads of celery, and throw all these into the broth with a good-sized handful of sweet herbs. Let all stew together for four hours and a half over a slow fire; strain off the liquid, take out the mutton, and force as much of the vegetables as possible through a coarse sieve with a wooden spoon, and return the pulp to the soup; beat up the yolks of two eggs with a quarter of a pint of cream, or milk, if you have not cream; stir all well together, and warm it up for sending to table.

sweet
herbs

CARROT SOUP

Take two quarts of stock, and to this add from six to ten carrots, according to the size, three turnips, three or four onions, and let them stew till tender. Then take out the vegetables, strain the soup, and with a spoon take off the red part of the carrots from the yellow centre, and force it through a coarse sieve; add the pulped carrot to the soup, till it is as thick as good cream; warm it, and serve at once.

PARSNIP SOUP

Take six large parsnips, two onions, and one good-sized head of celery. Cut them in pieces, and stew till tender in two quarts of light stock. Then take out the vegetables, pulp through a coarse sieve; return the pulp to the soup. Add a little white pepper, salt, and a pinch of sugar. Let it boil up, and just before serving add a quarter of a pint of cream.

VEGETABLE-MARROW SOUP

Slice down a large and somewhat old vegetable-marrow, two onions, a head of celery, and put them into a stewpan with two ounces of butter; stew ten minutes, then add three pints of stock, salt and pepper to taste, and let all boil gently till the vegetables are quite tender. Press them through a coarse sieve and heat the soup before sending to table. It should be made rather thick with the pulped vegetables.

45

GREEN-PEA SOUP

Take one quart (shelled) of old green peas, a head of celery, three lettuces, two onions, a small sprig of mint, a bunch of sweet herbs, and a quarter of a pound of lean ham or bacon, and let them boil till the peas are quite soft, in rather more than two quarts of stock, which need to be strong for this purpose; strain the soup from the meat and vegetables, press the latter with a wooden spoon through a sieve into the soup, add salt, a teaspoonful of pounded white sugar, and make it quite hot, putting in while doing so, sufficient spinach juice to give the soup a good green colour.

GREEN-PEA SOUP WITHOUT PEAS

Those who possess a kitchen garden can obtain this excellent soup early in the season, but only by sacrificing a part of a row of peas. When the plants are about eight inches high, cut off about three feet in the length of a row close to the ground, and boil them till the leaves are quite soft in three pints of stock, flavouring with salt and a little sugar; press all these through a sieve, and thicken the soup with a little flour and butter; give it a boil, and serve at once. This soup, though only made from the young leaves of the plants, will be found to have the same flavour as that given by the full-grown peas.

Hint: If the soup should not be well coloured, add spinach juice till sufficiently green.

47

JENNY LIND'S SOUP

Wash a quarter of a pound of the best pearl sago till the water poured from it is quite clear, then stew till nearly dissolved in water or broth; it will require a quart of liquid, which should be poured on it cold, and then heated very slowly. Then mix with it gradually a pint of good boiling cream, and the yolks of four eggs slightly beaten, and mingle the whole carefully with two quarts of strong and delicately flavoured stock, which should be kept ready boiling, and serve.

Fireproof Pot.

From The Dainty Housewife's Notebook...

Subsitute for New Potatoes
Cut old potatoes into very small balls, allow them to soak for three or four hours in cold water, then boil in cold water and serve with cream sauce. A very good substitute for new potatoes is obtained.

Wash Vegetables Well
Fruit and vegetable should be carefully washed before being eaten, as they often harbour countless micro-organisms.

MASHED PARSNIPS

Cut up the parsnips, boil them, mash, and press them through a coarse sieve; then put them into a stewpan with a little cream, pepper, and salt; stir them over the fire till quite hot, and then serve. If you have no cream, use instead a little milk, and a small piece of butter with a slight dredge of flour.

CARROTS WITH PARSLEY

Boil the carrots, and cut them in slices rather thicker than a penny piece; if very large, halve or quarter them down the length, before slicing. Take some sprigs of parsley, parboil and chop small; then put the sliced carrots into a pan with the chopped parsley, a good bit of butter and some pepper and salt; toss them over the fire till hot, and serve.

STEWED SPINACH

**wash
four
or five
times**

Carefully pick and wash the spinach four or five times in plenty of water, put it into a very large saucepan of boiling water with some salt, pressing down the leaves that rise above the water. When the spinach is half done, take it off the fire, strain it, and add to some fresh boiling water and salt. Boil again; the moment it is done, throw it into a colander, and pour cold water over it. Then make it into balls and press out every drop of water. Next chop it very fine till it becomes almost a paste. Put a lump of butter into a pan, place the spinach upon the butter, let it dry gently over the fire, and when the moisture is dried up, add a small quantity of good gravy with salt, pepper, a little nutmeg, and a small lump of sugar; let it boil up. Serve with neatly cut pieces of fried bread to garnish.

STEWED RED CABBAGE

Slice a middling-sized cabbage and put into a pan
with an onion sliced, pepper, salt, and half a pint
of gravy. Stew for two hours, then put in a bit of
butter mixed with a little flour, shake all well together, let it boil, and serve it quite hot.

STEWED PEAS

Handle the peas with butter in water and drain
them in a colander; put them into a pan with a
bundle of parsley and green onions, add half a wine-
glassful of water; let them sweat over a slow fire
until the peas are done. Add two large lumps of
sugar soaked in water. Take from the fire; when
off the boil, stir in the yolk of an egg, beaten up
with a table-spoonful of cold water, and serve.

CAULIFLOWER WITH CHEESE

Having boiled a fine cauliflower, prepare a sauce as follows:- into a quarter of a pound of butter rub a table-spoonful of flour, then put it into a stewpan, and as the butter melts, add by degrees half a pint of water, or a little more if you require more sauce; stir the whole till it boils and after a couple of minutes take it from the fire, and when entirely off the boil, add the yolk of an egg beaten up with a little lemon juice and a dessert-spoonful of soft water. Shake the stewpan till it is well mixed and the sauce set. Now powder the cauliflower rather thickly with rasped Parmesan cheese, then pour the sauce over it, and when the sauce is firmly set upon it, cover the surface with cheese, and then bread crumbs, and brown it with a salamander. Serve very hot, as a third-course dish.

POTATO CHIPS

Wash and pare off the skins of two or three or
more large potatoes, and when you have done this,
go on paring them, cutting them as thick and as
evenly as possible in ribbons nearly an inch wide;
throw these into boiling fat, let them take a nice
light colour, drain them well before the fire, and
serve immediately (or they lose their crispness)
piled high on a napkin.

They may be sent in with the game in the third
course.

Money-saving Ideas

—

Large savings are
generally effected
in small sums.

POTATOES A LA CRÊME

Put a piece of butter rolled in flour in a stewpan, with some salt, coarse pepper, and a little grated nutmeg; mix them well together, adding a large wine-glassful of cream, then place the sauce on the fire, and stir it round till it boils. Have ready some boiled potatoes cut in slices, put them into the sauce, and after warming them up, serve quite hot.

Hint: You may add to this sauce, if you wish, some green onions and a little chopped parsley.

NEW POTATOES AU BEURRE

Choosing the potatoes ...
Choose the potatoes as nearly of the same size as possible, wash them, and rub off the outer skin, then wipe them dry.

Prepare the butter ...

Put a quarter of a pound of fresh butter into a stewpan, set it on the fire, and when it boils throw in the potatoes; let them boil in the butter till they are done, taking care to toss them every now and then, so that they may all go successively into the boiling butter.

Keep a careful watch ...
They must be carefully watched, because if too much done they shrivel up and become waxy.

To serve ...
When the fork shows that they are done, they must
be taken out before they lose their crispness, put
into a dish, and some salt sprinkled over them.

To garnish ...
As soon as they are taken out of the boiling butter,
throw in a handful of parsley, and after it has had a
boil or two, lay it round the potatoes in the dish as
a garnish. They must be served immediately, as
they are spoiled by getting cold.

Hint: The butter in which the potatoes were boiled
may be poured into a jar, and will serve again for
the same purpose.

BEETROOT SALAD

Boil one or two large onions till soft and perfectly mild; when cold, pulp them through a sieve, and mix the onion with sliced beetroot and celery, adding salt, pepper, oil, and vinegar - the oil being in the proportion of three table-spoonfuls to one of vinegar. The onion and beetroot are very good without celery: the beetroot should be baked in the oven, which retains more flavour in than boiling.

TOMATO SALAD

Cut some tomatoes which are ripe without being too soft, in slices the thickness of a penny piece; sprinkle over them a small quantity of very finely chopped chives or green onions, add salt, pepper, oil, and vinegar, and serve with any roast meats.

HARICOT BEAN SALAD

Boil some small white haricot beans in water till quite tender, drain them well, and let them get quite cold. Chop up some tarragon, chervil, parsley and a little shalot together, all as small as possible. Put the cold haricot beans in a dish, sprinkle the chopped herbs over them, add salt, pepper, oil, and vinegar, mix all well together, and serve.

Salad Basket.

POTATO SALAD

Cold boiled potatoes make a very good salad, cutting them in slices a quarter of an inch thick, or rather less; lay them in a dish, sprinkle over them a little finely chopped parsley and chervil, adding salt, pepper, oil, and either plain or tarragon vinegar.

From The Dainty Housewife's Notebook...

Herbs

Herbs for kitchen use should be gathered on a dry day. Clean before drying in the heat of a stove; then pick off the leaves, chop, sift, and put into stoppered bottles. Label for use. Keep dry.

MINT.

From The Dainty Housewife's Notebook...

Herbs

Gather the different herbs in the months directed:

Basil ~ middle of August

Chervil ~ May, June and July

Fennel ~ May, June and July

Marjoram ~ July

Thyme ~ end of July and through August

Mint - end of June and July

Parsley ~ May, June and July

Sage ~ August and September

Tarragon ~ June, July and August.

Winter savoury ~ end of July and August.

BREAD SAUCE

Slice some white bread very thin and without crust, boil it in milk with a sliced onion and some whole white pepper; rub through a coarse sieve, return it to the stewpan, put in a small piece of butter, salt to taste, and a little cream if you have it, to make it of a proper thickness; warm sufficiently, and serve.

HORSERADISH SAUCE

Take a teaspoonful of mustard, and also of vinegar, three table-spoonfuls of thick cream, a very small quantity of shalot, a little salt, and grate as much horseradish into it as will make it as thick as onion sauce.

OYSTER SAUCE

Boil the oysters in their own liquor till they are   oysters
quite tender, and then beard them; mix with a knife
in a plate some butter with flour, and put into the
liquor strained; when it is hot, stir the oysters into
it, and add melted butter and a little cayenne pepper; give one boil, and the last thing add a squeeze
of lemon and serve.

THE EDIBLE OYSTER.

WHITE SAUCE

Take half a pint of cream or good milk, a quarter
of a pint of light-coloured stock, flavour with mace
or mushroom, a little salt, and thicken sufficiently
over the fire with a little flour and butter, and give
it a good boil.

LOBSTER SAUCE

lobster

Pick a lobster well, and cut the meat into small pieces; beat the spawn with a little cold butter in a marble mortar, mix with the pieces of lobster, and stir them into melted butter over the fire, and give the sauce one boil. A little cream is an improvement, and the sauce should be made the last thing before sending to table, as it is apt to separate.

BROWN ONION SAUCE

Slice some onions, and brown them in a stewpan in a little butter, then add a little good gravy or stock, and stew them till tender. This is an excellent sauce with rump steak.

From The Dainty Housewife's Notebook...

Baking Sponge Cake
For successful sponge cake, the flour should be sifted four times before measured, the sugar twice, and the tins should be lined with greased paper.

For Peeling Apples
Use a silver knife to peel apples, and the hands will not be blackened as when a steel knife is used. The acid of the fruit acts on the iron in the latter case, but does not affect the silver.

From The Dainty Housewife's Notebook...

The Salt Does It

When beating whites of eggs to a froth, always add a pinch of salt. The salt lowers the temperature, and makes them froth more easily.

Tinned Fruit

Opening tinned fruit an hour or two before using, that it may regain the excluded oxygen, improves the flavour. It should be turned at once into an earthen dish.

LEMON SOUFFLÉ

Put a pint and a half of milk into a stewpan with the rind of five lemons and one ounce of isinglass, and let it boil ten minutes; beat up the yolks of eight eggs, and when the milk is nearly cold mix them with it and put it on the fire to thicken; take it off, and as soon as it cools, stir in the whites of the eggs which you have whipped to a stiff froth, half a pound of powdered sugar, the juice of the lemons, and about three ounces of pistachio nuts chopped fine.

Oil your mould, sprinkle it with some of the chopped pistachio nuts, then pour the soufflé carefully in; place it in ice or in a cold place to set it, then turn it out of the mould, and serve.

ORANGE JELLY

Squeeze a sufficient number of oranges to give a pint and a half of juice. Pare the rind of two oranges and one lemon very thin, and put them into a stewpan with half a pint of water, and let it boil till all the flavour is gone from the peels into the water, then strain it off and dissolve in it over the fire one ounce of gelatine or isinglass and half a pound of sugar; when dissolved and nearly cold pour into it the orange juice, stir it thoroughly till mixed.

Pour it into an oiled mould, and place it on ice or in a cold place till set.

Fancy Jelly.

RED ROBIN

Take one pound and a half of lump sugar, and put it into a stewpan with a pint of water and boil till it becomes thick; then add two pounds of apples, peeled and cored, and the rind of a large lemon cut thin, and boil all together till it is quite stiff, stirring it frequently; then pour it into an oiled mould, and when cold turn it out, and serve with a rich custard, or it is very good alone.

Hint: Stirring frequently prevents burning.

APPLE WHIP

Take twelve large apples, bake them quite soft, pulp them through a sieve, sweeten to taste, and flavour with lemon rind rubbed on sugar; whip well then add the whites of two eggs. Continue whipping for three-quarters of an hour.

The quantity, which will fill a pint basin before it is whipped, would fill a large colander after the whisking, and should be as white as snow.

Pile it high in a glass dish, and serve at once.

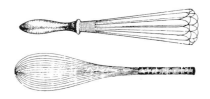

SLIP CURD

Take half a tumbler of sherry, a quarter of a pound of loaf sugar, half the rind of a lemon cut very thin, and on the other half rub some of the lumps of sugar to give more flavour, mix this till the sugar is all dissolved. From a quart of milk take a cupful and warm it sufficiently with a piece of rennet the size of a nutmeg, to make the rest of the milk luke-warm when added to it. Put the wine &c., into a glass dish, pour the milk upon it, first taking out the rennet (which must be well washed before it is put into the milk).

When the curd is sufficiently set and cold, send it to the table.

half a
tumbler
of sherry

73

STANDING CUSTARD

Take a pint of new milk, set it on the fire, and when it boils have ready the yolks of six eggs and two ounces of loaf-sugar well beaten; whip them in the milk, and then set it on the fire again, but do not let it boil; then whip it till nearly cold, and add half an ounce of isinglass well dissolved and beat it again till thick enough to put into the oiled mould: fill it with the custard, and let it stand till next day, then turn it out, and pour the following sauce over it: make a thinnish syrup with some fine loaf sugar, cut the peel of a lemon into very fine chips, when the sugar is boiling, squeeze in some lemon juice, and when luke-warm throw in the chips.

As soon as it is quite cold, pour it over the custard before it is sent to table.

CUSTARD

Take one pint of milk and half a pint of cream, the yolks of eight eggs well beaten, the thin rind of a lemon, six bitter almonds (pounded), sugar to taste, and a glass of brandy; put all into a large jug, and place in a saucepan of boiling water, keep on stirring one way as soon as your custard becomes hot and begins to thicken; and when sufficiently thick, instantly take it off the fire, or it will curdle, and keep stirring till it cools.

Do not add the brandy till you take it off the fire, when you must remove the lemon-rind. When cold, send to table in a glass dish or custard cups.

ORANGE CUSTARD

Boil the rind of half a Seville orange till very tender, and beat it in a mortar till quite smooth; put to it a table-spoonful of brandy, the juice of a Seville orange, four ounces of loaf-sugar and the yolks of four eggs. Beat this mixture well together for ten minutes, and then pour in by degrees a pint of boiling cream or new milk; keep beating the whole time till cold, then pour into custard cups.

Set them in a deep dish of hot water, and let them stand till they are set.

Money-saving Ideas
—

To make savings,
buy provisions in large
quantities and take proper
care that they are not wasted.

RICE CHEESECAKES

Take a quarter of a pound of finely sifted ground rice, a quarter of a pound of sifted loaf sugar, a quarter of a pound of fresh butter beaten to a cream, and the yolks of four eggs; the eggs and sugar must be well beaten together, then the butter and rice added, the whites of the eggs beaten separately; mix all together, and flavour with a small blade of mace, finely pounded, and a table-spoonful of rose-water, or the peel of two lemons rubbed on sugar.
The quicker this is made, the lighter the cheesecakes will be; the batter should be poured into little tartlet tins, not quite full, and baked in a brisk oven. Serve them cold.

GOOSEBERRY FOOL

THE GOOSEBERRY.

Take a quart of green gooseberries, put them into a deep dish, and bake them in the oven till quite soft, then pulp them through a coarse sieve, and add pounded sugar to taste; when cold, stir in a gill of cream, mix thoroughly, and serve in a glass dish or custard cups.

CURRANT FOOL

Stew ripe red currants with sufficient sugar to sweeten them, and when done pulp them through a coarse sieve, and add sufficient cream and very fine bread crumbs to make it thick enough.
Serve when cold in custard cups or a glass dish.

STEWED PLUMS

If the plums are not very dry, an hour's soaking in cold water will be sufficient, but if they are old they should be put to soak over night. Make a thin syrup, and put in some fine shreds of lemon-peel, then stew the plums in the syrup in a stewpan closely covered for about three hours till quite tender, and while stewing add a glass of white wine. When cold, serve in a glass dish, with cream or custard to eat with them.

Money-saving Ideas
—
It is a false economy
to buy bad food.

FRUIT SALAD

Thinly peel two oranges, then rub the oil from them on some lump sugar; add the rind in a stewpan, with a little water to make a syrup. Add the juice of a lemon, strain out the rinds, and set the syrup by to get cold. Peel some apples and oranges (carefully taking off every scrape of white peel) then take whatever nice preserved fruits you have, such as dried cherries, whole strawberries, raspberries, pieces of pineapple, angelica, cucumber, apricot, &c. Pile them up in a glass dish, with the pieces of oranges and apples, mixing as you go. Then peel two more oranges, cut them nicely in quarters, and place on the top with some of your best fruits; then pour over first the orange syrup, and lastly two table-spoonfuls of curaçao or noyau. It should not stand long after making before it is sent to table.

From The Dainty Housewife's Notebook...

When Cutting Cake
Before cutting a cake, the knife should be warmed,
and the cake will be found to cut much easier.

To Keep Nuts Fresh
To keep nuts fresh throughout the year they should
be packed in casks between layers of fine sand.

OATMEAL CAKES

Melt four ounces of lard or butter, and mix it with seven ounces of fine oatmeal, five ounces of pastry flour, and three ounces of caster sugar, which have been all blended. Break the egg into a little cold water, beat it slightly and stir it with the other ingredients so as to make a stiff paste. Turn the paste on to a board, roll it out very thin, and cut into large square pieces, and scatter dry oatmeal over. Grease a large baking-sheet and bake cakes in a slow oven from twenty to thirty minutes.

Money-saving Ideas
—
Savings should be made
in indulgences and not
in necessities.

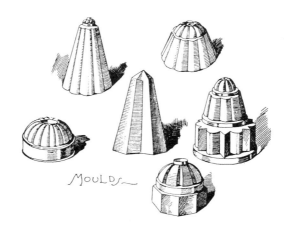

MOULDS

From The Dainty Housewife's Notebook...

Useful stale bread

Stale bread is a never-ending source of supply to the economical cook, yet, with the best intentions, it will sometimes accumulate. There are some useful recipes to help dispose of it, all of which are worth trying.

Useful bread and butter

Bread and butter left over is even more difficult than bread to utilise. The thrifty cook will learn to make bread and jam fritters.

STEAMED MARMALADE PUDDING

Take half a pound of stale pieces of bread and rub them through a sieve. Chop a quarter of a pound of beef suet very finely. Grate the rind of one lemon on to them.

Put six table-spoonfuls of marmalade in the basin, strain in the juice of the lemon, break up an egg, add it with half a gill of milk and beat all well together; then add the crumbs, suet and two ounces of mixed peel. Well grease a pudding basin, put in the mixture, pressing it down, twist a piece of greased paper round the top of the basin, put the basin in a saucepan with boiling water to come half-way up it, and steam the pudding for two and a half hours. Then take off the paper, turn the pudding on to a hot dish, sprinkle a little caster sugar on the top, and pour round some marmalade sauce.

From The Dainty Housewife's Notebook...

The Art of Making Bread Crumbs
To ensure bread crumbs are all of the same size, rub them through a sieve; if made on a grater they are generally of uneven proportion.

BREAD AND JAM FRITTERS

First prepare the batter. Sieve four ounces of flour and a level teaspoonful of salt into a basin. Break an egg into the middle of it, pour on to it about two table-spoonfuls of milk, then with a wooden spoon work in the flour gradually; next add a little more milk, and beat the batter well, until the surface is covered with bubbles, then add the rest of the milk. Cut the slices of bread and butter into neat pieces, spread one piece with a little stoneless jam, lay on a second piece, and press them together. Have ready a pan of frying fat. When a faint bluish smoke rises from it, coat a piece of bread and jam with the batter, then drop it into the fat and fry a pretty golden brown. Drain it well on paper, then dust with caster sugar. When all the pieces are fried, serve them neatly arranged on a hot dish.

HINTS WORTH REMEMBERING

When selecting fish in a shop, it is important to observe:
The eyes are full and bright.
The gills are clear, bright red.
The body is stiff.
The flesh is firm and elastic to the touch.
The smell is fresh, not unpleasant.
Girth is large in comparison to length. Very large fish should be avoided, since it is probable that they are old and that the fibres are stringy.

HINTS WORTH REMEMBERING

The experienced cook well knows that a reasonable
amount of meat, augmented with a well-flavoured
thick gravy, plenty of vegetables or other garnish,
will go as far again as slices of cold joint, and give
also greater satisfaction and superior nutriment.

HINTS WORTH REMEMBERING

Take advantage of the season of the year, making the most of the many excellent cold dishes when the thermometer registers ninety degrees Fahrenheit in the shade and paying them scant attention when it falls below zero.

THE SERVANTLESS HOUSEHOLD
HOW TO COPE – SOME POLITE ADVICE
How to keep the house in order without the benefit of staff. Maintain high standards and be prepared for anything! Includes essential 'Don'ts and Buts'.

APPEARANCES
HOW TO KEEP THEM UP
ON A LIMITED INCOME
Use the housekeeping money wisely, train the cook well, how to shop, how to plan a modest dinner party.

Dainty Dishes for slender incomes

KITCHEN COSMETICS
BEAUTY FROM YOUR PANTRY
How to have a smooth, clear complexion –
and other potions and preparations for
natural beauty.
Original ingredients from yesterday's
kitchens.

For your free catalogue containing these and other
titles write to:

Copper Beech Publishing Ltd
P O Box 159 East Grinstead
Sussex England RH19 4FS
www.copperbeechpublishing.co.uk

Copper Beech Gift Books
are designed and printed in
Great Britain.